Other giftbooks in this series
Sorry
Go Girl!
I love you madly

Printed simultaneously in 2005 by Helen Exley Giftbooks in Great Britain
and Helen Exley Giftbooks LLC in the USA.

Illustrations © Caroline Gardner Publishing, Liz Smith and Helen Exley 2005
Text © Helen Exley 2005
Written by Pam Brown, with extra entries by Pamela Dugdale, Marion C. Garretty
and Jane Swan.

Selection and arrangement copyright © Helen Exley 2005
The moral right of the author has been asserted.

ISBN 1-905130-74-0 | 12 11 10·9 8 7 6 5 4 3 2

A copy of the CIP data is available from the British Library on request.
All rights reserved. No part of this publication may be reproduced in any form
or by any means without permission.

Edited by Helen Exley
Pictures by Liz Smith and Caroline Gardner

Printed in China

Helen Exley Giftbooks, 16 Chalk Hill, Watford, Herts WD19 4BG, UK
Helen Exley Giftbooks LLC, 185 Main Street, Spencer MA 01562, USA
www.helenexleygiftbooks.com

Little things mean a lot

by Pam Brown

A HELEN EXLEY GIFTBOOK

Such a small thing.
A little cutting in a little pot
that will spread its leaves
and scent the air
for years to come.

You made no dramatic gestures,
gave no solemn lectures –
you simply made the tea
and fetched the biscuit tin.

Small surprises

– a bunch of raggedy flowers on the
  doorstep to start my day.
A fairy cake with a candle in the icing on
  my birthday.
The book that I'd been searching for.
        Fruit out of season.
A ginger kitten.
        – How did you know?

Kindness is given so softly,
so gently, falling like tiny seeds
along our path – and brightening it
with flowers.

You know a silly postcard
      on a Monday morning brightens
the day – the heart. The Universe!

            Kindness can be a postcard,
         a phone call, a bunch of flowers,
            a word of thanks,
                  a cup of tea,
            a lift in the car,
         a trip to the chemist.
            A listening ear.

You dropped in for a chat,
washed a few dishes, fed the cat.
Matched the knitting skein.
Climbed those long stairs up
to the lonely flat.
You did these things for me
when I was in trouble,
eased fear and pain.
Thank you for that.

It is the net of small kindnesses
that holds humanity together.

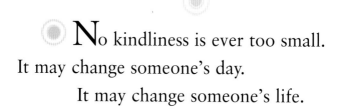

No kindliness is ever too small.
It may change someone's day.
It may change someone's life.

You give me your time -

Those who give most help
are those who stay around
after the first burst of sympathy is over.

he most generous gift of all.

You emailed
because you haven't seen me for a while
and are worried about me.
Thanks.
I was fine.
Just busy.
But it's wonderful to be worried about.

Great acts of generosity
and assistance are vital
in this dangerous world.
But so are the small, concerned kindnesses
that reassure the lonely heart.

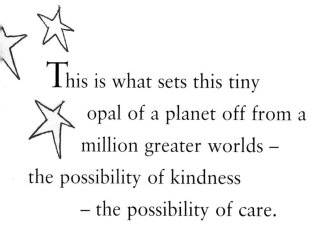

This is what sets this tiny
opal of a planet off from a
million greater worlds –
the possibility of kindness
– the possibility of care.

For quiet laughter over coffee.
For enraptured laughter at a show.
For explosive laughter at the bar.
Thank you.
Laughter with a friend
sets a person free.

I was reduced to melancholy
by unkindness –
you picked me up,
dusted me down and
restored my confidence and hope.

There are the people
  we called Ordinary,
      Dull, Conventional –
who weave a mesh of little
    kindnesses that holds
        the world together.

Thank you
for being there when I was
   embarking on something idiotic –
and waiting around to
   pick up the pieces without once
   saying "I told you so".

You like to hear about
the ordinary things in my life.
Just because it's me. I'm very grateful –
you're a great audience!

Thank you
for looking out for
    something that would
enchant me –
    silly,
beautiful
    and wonderfully useful.

You taught me what it feels like
to be cared for. That is
a most wonderful gift.

This greeting is not just from me –
but from the garden birds you feed
and the cats you stroke and the dogs you talk to;
from the small, wild four-footed things
you help through the very cold winters.
From the trees you prune
and the seedlings that you nurture.
From the people who are cheered by your smile.
From all the lives you touch and brighten.

I love it that you always know

when not to help.

Yºou and I
– our friendship is stitched
together by
small kindnesses.
Apples from the garden.
A cup of sugar when
the jar is empty.
A magazine.
A cup of tea on a dreary day.
Mutual affection.
Mutual concern.

Thank you

for knowing when to be silent.

When to simply hold my hand.

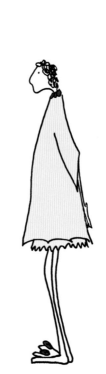

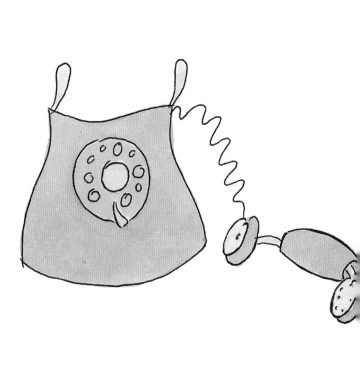

The day started badly.

It was raining.

The milkman had forgotten to call.

The postman hadn't.

A fistful of bills.

A drift of circulars.

Gloom.

Doom.

But then you rang.

And made me laugh.

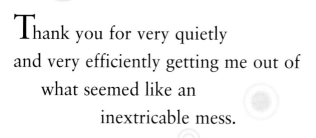

Thank you for very quietly
and very efficiently getting me out of
what seemed like an
inextricable mess.

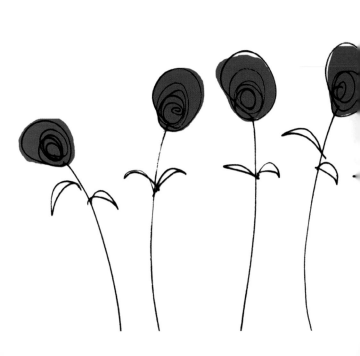

I felt myself a failure,
inadequate, stupid, a nothing creature –
you did not turn away, exasperated by my gloom,
but lured me back to life.
OK, you seemed to say.
So you're not in line
for a Nobel Prize.
And the exam results were
nothing like you hoped...
And I gave a watery grin –
and rejoined
the human race.

The truly kind
don't offer to carry your carrier bags.
They simply take them from you.

You write or phone or
turn up on the doorstep –
and make me feel
I'm necessary to someone.
Thank you for that.

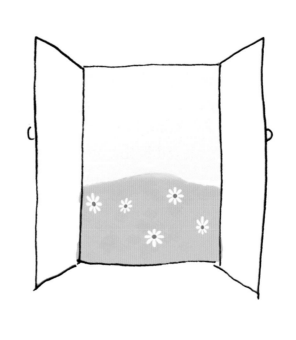

The kind heart
understands a need before it's spoken –
and answers it so quietly
it seems coincidence.

You didn't just give me a lift
    because you were going my way.
You turned your car round
    and asked me where I was going.

A phone call.

No real reason.

Just to make sure that I'm all right.

Bless you.

Passion is splendid, but...
the small reassuring touch,
the little kiss in passing,
the smile,
the daft surprise
– these are what endure
and make my life a joy.

The long, long memories are o

people who were kind.

I gather up all the little things
that have astonished and
enchanted me.
They crown my
days in joy.

I suppose I could have
struggled through without you.
But thank heavens
I didn't have to.

Thank you for simply being you – constant

We cherish the remembrance
of small kindnesses
when much else has been forgotten.

friendship, unfailing in kindness.

My garden is bright
with plants that
you gave me.
Your friendship blossoming.

Such sma

things comfort the heart.

A ladybird.

A drift of autumn leaves.

A shaft of sunlight.

A smile.

Helen Exley runs her own publishing company
which sells giftbooks in more than seventy countries.
Helen's books cover the many events and emotions in life,
and she was eager to produce a book to say a simple 'sorry'.
Caroline Gardner's delightfully quirky 'elfin' cards
provided the inspiration Helen needed to go ahead
with this idea, and from there this series of stylish
and witty books quickly grew:
Sorry, *Go Girl!*, *I love you madly*, and *Little things mean a lot*.

Caroline Gardner Publishing has been producing beautifully
designed stationery from offices overlooking the River Thames
in England since 1993 and has been developing the destinctive
'elfin' stationery range over the last five years.
There are also several new illustrations created especially for
these books by freelance artist and designer Liz Smith.

Pam Brown has worked with Helen Exley for over fifteen
years. She has contributed to dozens of books, including the
best-selling *To-Give-and-To-Keep*® range.